SO YOU THINK YOU'RE A BASEBALL FAN

What Every Knowledgeable Baseball Fan Should Know

by
Jack Clary

Quinlan Press
Boston

Published by Quinlan Press
131 Beverly Street
Boston, MA 02114

Cover design and illustration by Joe Bergin

All photographs courtesy of the National Baseball Library,
Cooperstown, New York

ISBN 1-55770-058-3

Printed in the United States of America
May 1988

To my nephew, J. T. Roman, the noblest Fordham Ram of them all, who found a special joy in baseball from the first moment he heard horsehide hit ash.

I would like to thank Pat Kelly of the Hall of Fame for her help in providing the photographs for this book.

Jack Clary is a free-lance sports media specialist and author of over two dozen sports books, including *Baseball's Signs and Signals*, *Minnesota Twins Trivia* and *Once a Giant, Always. . .*, with Andy Robustelli. For fifteen years he was a sportswriter and columnist for the Associated Press, the *New York World Telegram* and the *Boston Herald Traveler.*

Contents

History

1. What player was the first black ever to win the AL's MVP award?

2. When the Dodgers left Brooklyn for the West Coast after the 1957 season, where did they play their home games?

3. What famous baseball pioneer was a graduate of the U.S. Military Academy?

4. Who was the first black umpire in the major leagues?

5. What players formed the double play combination for the Yankees' great teams of 1926, 1927 and 1928?

6. In 1947 did Ted Williams or Joe DiMaggio win the AL's Most Valuable Player award by one point?

A. A runner is at third base and the hitter has an 0-2 count on him when the manager signals for a steal home. As the runner breaks, the pitcher legally steps back off the rubber and fires home. The batter did not see him back off the rubber, swings at the ball and hits it into the center for a hit. What is the ruling?

**These challenging rules questions are scattered throughout the book. The answers are contained in the second-last chapter.*

7. What was the original name of the Houston Astros?

8. Who was the first designated hitter to appear officially in an American League game?

9. Though the Brooklyn Dodgers won the 1947 National League pennant, who was the player who could only finish fourth—the highest by any Brooklyn player—in the NL MVP race?

10. Who holds the major league record for grounding into the most double plays?
    a) Jim Rice
    b) Hank Aaron
    c) Maury Wills
    d) Harmon Killebrew

11. "Spahn, Sain, and pray for rain" was the rallying cry of what National League team in 1948?

12. In 1969 the Phils traded Rich Allen, Cookie Rojas and Jerry Johnson to the Cardinals for Tim McCarver, Byron Browne, Joe Hoerner and one other player, who refused to report and brought a suit that ultimately led to free agency in major league baseball. Who was that player?

13. Who was the New York Giants hitter who smacked a home run still known as "the hit heard 'round the world," and why did it get the monicker?

B.	Two outs, score tied, runners on first and third, and the batter loops a hit into the outfield that falls just in front of the leftfielder. The runner on third trots home, but the runner on first, thinking there is only one out, doesn't reach second base before the fielder's throw gets him on a forceout. Does the run count?

14. Which National League teams share the record for hitting the most homers in a single season?
   a) 1975 Cincinnati Reds d) 1956 Cincinnati Reds
   b) 1947 New York Giants e) 1980 Philadelphia Phils
   c) 1955 Brooklyn Dodgers f) 1926 Pittsburgh Pirates

15. What major league team holds the season record for hitting the most home runs?
   a) 1961 Yankees
   b) 1949 Red Sox
   c) 1975 Reds
   d) 1983 Phillies

16. What major league team holds the record for the most consecutive victories?

17. Babe Ruth was famed as a home run hitter, but who was the "Babe" who hit the first home run in a major league night game?

18. Pitcher Lefty Grove gained his greatest fame as a strike-out artist *en route* to the Hall of Fame, but he also established a "first" in what other strike-out category?

19. John B. McLean was a member of the Boston Red Sox in 1901, but he is best remembered (if at all) for what pioneering feat on April 26 of that year?

20. What pioneer hitting feat did Lou Gehrig accomplish during his time with the famed "Murderer's Row" of the New York Yankees?

C. Man on second and third, one out, score tied in the bottom of the ninth inning: the hitter drives the ball over the rightfielder's head, and the ball bounces into the stands. Of course the runner from third scores the winning run, but is the hitter given credit for a ground rule double and does the runner on second score, too?

21. In these days of the lively ball, we should pay particular homage to Roscoe Barnes and Charles Jones of the National League, and Erwin Beck of the American League for what reason?

22. What catcher appeared in the most regular-season games in major league history?

23. What is the origin of the baseball term "rookie"?

24. Who was the former major league general manager of the Indians, Cardinals, A's and White Sox who earned the nickname "Trader" because of the 400-plus trades that he engineered?

25. Which pair of third basemen became the first at their position to be chosen their respective league's MVPs in the same season?

26. What was Lou Gehrig's streak of games played con-

This stadium was the home for managers Joe McCarthy, Bucky Harris and Casey Stengel during the forties.

**Photographs of classic ballparks are spread throughout the book. If you cannot identify them all, check out the answers on the final pages of the book.*

secutively, when did it begin and when did it end?

27. Since 1908, they've been known as the Chicago Cubs, but prior to that they had 16 nicknames. Can you name half of them and why the team settled on Cubs?

D.	Bunting foul with two strikes is an automatic strikeout, but suppose a runner on first base takes off on the pitch and steals second. Is he given a steal on the strikeout?

28. Who was the pitcher for the Mets and Red Sox who was credited with the victory in a 33-inning game—longest pro game ever—while pitching for Pawtucket of the International League?

29. In 1975 the Cleveland Indians signed what former player as the major league's first black manager?
   a) Hank Aaron
   b) Jackie Robinson
   c) Frank Robinson
   d) Tommy Harper

30. Can you name the three players from the list below who played 25 seasons in the major leagues during the twentieth century?

Eddie Collins	Ted Williams
Pete Rose	Willie Mays
Lou Gehrig	Jim Kaat
Tommy John	Phil Niekro

31. Jackie Robinson was the first black player in the major leagues, but who was the first black player to hit a home run in the American League?

32. If you love baseball, then you would have enjoyed the longest

game ever played in the majors. What teams played? Where was the game and what was the final score?

33. The old saw, "You can't tell the players' numbers without a program," didn't sell in the American League until the season when which team finally numbered the back of their jerseys?

34. Night games have become so commonplace that a day game now is a happening, but can you name the year, the teams and the site at which the first night game was played?

E. There is a runner on first base, no outs and a new pitcher enters the game. He promptly picks off the baserunner before throwing a single pitch to the batter. He now has been credited with one-third of an inning but has not pitched to a batter. Can he be removed from the game for another pitcher?

35. The Yankees and Mets occupy New York City now, but there have also been four other major league teams in the city. Name them.

36. Throughout their careers, the following players were always called by their nicknames. Match them with their given names.

Dixie Walker	Frank
Sparky Lyle	Stanley
Preacher Roe	Russell
Satchel Paige	Albert
Tug McGraw	Elwin
Bucky Dent	Fred
Bucky Harris	Leroy

37. Name the four players who are tied for the most American League MVP awards.

38. Name the two players who have won the most MVP awards in the National League.

39. Match the year and the player who won the National League Rookie of the Year award:

1980	Dwight Gooden
1981	Fernando Valenzuela
1982	Vince Coleman
1983	Steve Howe
1984	Todd Worrell
1985	Benito Santiago
1986	Darryl Strawberry
1987	Steve Sax

40. Match the year and the American League Rookie of the Year:

1980	Ozzie Guillen
1981	Dave Righetti
1982	Mark McGwire
1983	Alvin Davis
1984	Jose Canseco
1985	Cal Ripken, Jr.
1986	Joe Charboneau
1987	Ron Kittle

41. Match the year and the player who won the American League's Most Valuable Player award:

1980	Willie Hernandez
1981	Roger Clemens
1982	Rollie Fingers
1983	George Brett
1984	Don Mattingly
1985	George Bell
1986	Robin Yount
1987	Cal Ripken, Jr.

F.	A catcher running toward the stands to catch a foul ball has his hat in his open hand, misjudges the ball, and the ball lands in his hat. The ruling?

42. Match the year and the player who won the National League's Most Valuable Player (Note: There are two multiple winners):

1980	Willie McGee
1981	Mike Schmidt
1982	Dale Murphy
1983	Andre Dawson
1984	Ryne Sandberg
1985	
1986	
1987	

43. Who was the last Yankees player to wear uniform number 3 before it was retired in honor of Babe Ruth?

44. Match the names and retired uniform numbers of these Hall-of-Famers:

Willie McCovey	6
Earl Averill	20
Duke Snider	44
Roberto Clemente	3
Al Kaline	4
Yogi Berra	21
Jackie Robinson	42
Lou Brock	8

45. When Ronald Reagan was a movie actor, he played which Hall-of-Famer in *The Winning Team*?
    a) Grover Cleveland Alexander
    b) Waite Hoyt
    c) Walter Johnson
    d) Lefty Grove

Outfielder Bobby Thomson hit a 1951 playoff-winning home run, the "shot heard 'round the world," against the Dodgers in this park.

46. So much for experience, but which of the Hall-of-Famers listed below never played in the minor leagues?

Mel Ott	Ted Williams
Bob Feller	Sandy Koufax
Bob Gibson	Al Kaline
Joe DiMaggio	Frankie Frisch

G. In Game 4 of the 1980 NL championship, Pete Rose was on third base and Mike Schmidt on first for the Phils when Manny Trillo hit a sacrifice fly to the left, on which the fielder made a diving catch. Rose tagged and scored, but Schmidt, thinking the ball was trapped, never retouched the base before heading for second base. The Astros catcher threw to first base and Schmidt was declared out, completing a double play, but the run still counted. Why?

Answers

1. b) Elston Howard of the 1963 Yankees was the first black player ever to win the MVP award in the American League.

2. b) Los Angeles Coliseum, until Dodgers Stadium was built in 1962

3. Abner Doubleday, the father of American baseball

4. Emmet Ashford, starting in 1966

5. Shortstop Mark Koeniz and second baseman Tony Lazzeri

6. DiMaggio edged Williams, 202–201, for the MVP award.

7. The Colt .45s

8. Ron Blomberg of the Yankees was walked by Red Sox pitcher Luis Tiant in the top of the first inning on April 6, 1973. Others DHs appeared that day, but on the clock Blomberg was number one.

9. Catcher Bruce Edwards. Third baseman Bob Elliott of the Boston Braves won the award.

10. b) Hank Aaron grounded into 328 DPs during his career.

11. The Boston Braves, who won the NL pennant that year

12. Curt Flood

13. Bobby Thomson's three-run homer in the last of the ninth inning of an NL pennant playoff game brought the Giants the 1951 National League pennant, and capped an incredible drive that overhauled the Brooklyn Dodgers.

14. The 1947 New York Giants and 1956 Cincinnati Reds share the NL club homer record of 221.

15. a) The 1961 New York Yankees hit 240 homers.

16. The New York Giants won 26 games in a row in 1926.

17. Floyd (Babe) Herman for Cincinnati on July 10, 1935.

18. Grove was the first AL player to strike out five times in a nine-inning game.

19. McLean was the first pinch-hitter in American League history, and then got the first pinch hit, a double, during that at-bat.

20. He was the first AL player ever to hit four home runs in a nine-inning game, June 3, 1932.

21. Barnes and Jones were the first NL players to hit home runs, on May 2, 1876; Beck was the first in the AL, on April 25, 1901.

22. Bob Boone

23. It came from the Army term for an untrained recruit.

24. Frank (Trader) Lane

25. c) Robinson and Boyer. Brett and Schmidt were the second.

26. Gehrig played in 2,130 consecutive games, beginning on June 1, 1925, and ending on May 3, 1939.

27. At one time that Chicago entry was known as the White Stockings, Colts, Black Stockings, Ex-Colts, Rainmakers, Orphans, Cowboys, Rough Riders, Desert Rangers, Remnants, Recruits, Zephyrs, Nationals, Spuds and Trojans. Cubs came about when the new American League entry raided the roster in 1902, taking the good vets but not the younger players—the cubs.

28. Bobby Ojeda, who pitched just one inning on the second day of the game. . .65 days after the first 32 innings were played on April 18–19, 1981

29. c) Frank Robinson

30. Eddie Collins, Tommy John and Jim Kaat

31. Willard Brown of the St. Louis Browns hit a pinch-hit,

inside-the-park HR on August 17, 1947, the same season that Robinson broke the color line in the National League.

32. The Brooklyn Dodgers and Boston Braves played a 1-1, 26-inning tie on May 1, 1920 (and did it in less time than some nine-inning games take today).

33. In 1929 the Yankees were the first team in the AL ever to have numbers on their jerseys.

34. Cincinnati beat Philadelphia, 2-1, on May 24, 1935, at Cincinnati.

35. New York Mutuals (1876), New York Giants (1883), Brooklyn Dodgers (1890) and New York Highlanders (now Yankees) (1903)

36. Fred (Dixie) Walker, Albert (Sparky) Lyle, Elwin (Preacher) Roe, Leroy (Satchel) Paige, Frank (Tug) McGraw, Russell (Bucky) Dent and Stanley (Bucky) Harris

37. Jimmie Foxx, Joe DiMaggio, Yogi Berra and Mickey Mantle each won three MVP awards in the AL.

38. Mike Schmidt and Roy Campanella have each won three NL MVP awards.

39. 1980—Howe; 1981—Valenzuela; 1982—Sax; 1983—Strawberry; 1984—Gooden; 1985—Coleman; 1986—Worrell; 1987—Santiago

40. 1980—Charboneau; 1981—Righetti; 1982—Ripken; 1983—Kittle; 1984—Davis; 1985—Guillen; 1986—Canseco; 1987—McGwire

This park was located next to Coogan's Bluff in New York City.

41. 1980—Brett; 1981—Fingers; 1982—Yount; 1983—Ripken; 1984—Hernandez; 1985—Mattingly; 1986—Clemens; 1987—Bell

42. 1980—Schmidt; 1981—Schmidt; 1982—Murphy; 1983—Murphy; 1984—Sandberg; 1985—McGee; 1986—Schmidt; 1987—Sandberg

43. Cliff Mapes, an outfielder

44. McCovey—44; Averill—3; Snider—4; Clemente—21; Kaline—6; Berra—8; Robinson—42; Brock—20

45. a) Grover Cleveland Alexander

46. Ott, Feller, Koufax, Kaline and Frisch

World Series

1. It is the sixth game of the 1975 World Series. In the eighth inning the Red Sox get the first two batters on base. Rawley Eastwick comes on in relief for Cincinnati, gets the next two hitters, and has a 2-2 count on pinch-hitter Bernie Carbo. Why was Carbo batting and what did he do on the next pitch?

2. Who made the final out when Don Larsen pitched his perfect game in the 1956 World Series against the Brooklyn Dodgers?

3. Who are the only two pitchers ever to hit a World Series home run in their first at-bat?

Sandy Koufax	Jose Santiago
Jim Beattie	Eddie Plank
Jim Palmer	Burleigh Grimes
Mickey Lolich	Jim Kaat

4. Who is the only pitcher ever to hit a grand-slam home run

in the World Series?

5. Since the World Series went to a seven-game format, five teams have come from a 1-3 deficit to win. Name them.

6. Which was the first expansion (post 1962) team ever to win a World Series, and what team did it beat?

H.	With two outs and a man on second, the batter hits a drive between the rightfielder and centerfielder that scores the baserunner and goes for an inside-the-park home run. The defense appeals that the hitter did not touch first base, and he is called out. Does the runner who was on second score?

7. Which major league team has appeared in the most World Series and come away with the most championships?
   a) New York Yankees
   b) Brooklyn/Los Angeles Dodgers
   c) New York/San Francisco Giants
   d) Chicago Cubs

8. Who was the Dodgers player who spoiled Floyd Bevens's bid for a no-hitter in the 1947 World Series, and how did he do it?

9. Who was the only player ever to pitch in both the Little League World Series and the World Series?

10. Which major league has won the most World Series, through 1987?

11. Who was the Pirates' second baseman who hit a 1960 World Series-winning home run, and against what pitcher was it hit?

12. Who was on deck in that 1960 World Series game when the winning home run was hit?

13. Which team led the major leagues in stolen bases during the regular season, yet never stole one during its seven-game World Series victory?

I.	With a runner on first, the batter hits a ground ball to the second baseman, who fields it with his glove, removes the ball and tags the runner with the empty glove. Is the runner out?

14. Who was the Chicago Cubs pitcher in the 1932 World Series against whom Babe Ruth hit his famous called shot home run?

15. What Giants hitter had his line drive caught with a leaping grab by Yankees second baseman Bobby Richardson, choking off a San Francisco rally and giving the Yanks the World Series title in 1962?

16. Who hit the game-winning double, and who did it score for the game-winning run in the St. Louis Cardinals' seventh game World Series victory over the Red Sox in 1946?

17. True or false: Ty Cobb's World Series average was below .300.

18. Who was the first player ever to win a World Series game, 1-0, with a home run?

19. Who was the oldest pitcher ever to hurl a complete game in the World Series?

20. What player played for six pennant-winning teams but never

got into the World Series with those teams?

J. If a ball hits the third-base bag and bouces backward and into foul territory, what is the call?

21. Who is the only Olympic Gold Medal winner ever to appear in a World Series?

22. Who was the only PGA tournament winner ever to play in a World Series?

23. Who was the only manager's wife ever to sing the National Anthem before a World Series game?

24. Who was the only coach ever to win an NFL championship and also appear in a World Series?

25. Which pitcher accumulated the most shutouts in World Series history?
    a) Christy Mathewson
    b) Sandy Koufax
    c) Walter Johnson
    d) Cy Young

26. Who was the Milwaukee Braves pitcher who beat the New York Yankees with three complete games in the 1957 World Series, including the deciding seventh game?

27. Who are the only four players ever to play on a winning World Series team, manage one and win a batting title?

When the New York Giants moved to the West Coast in 1958, they played in this stadium.

K.	With two out and a runner on third base, the batter swings and misses at strike three, but the ball gets past the catcher and rolls to the backstop. The runner on third streaks for home while the catcher is retrieving the ball, but the batter falls on the way to first base and the catcher throws the ball to first base before he gets there. Does the run count?

28. Who played in 50 World Series games and never hit a home run?
    a) Jack Saltzgaver
    b) Frankie Frisch
    c) Sal Maglie
    d) Yogi Berra

29. Who was the sore-armed pitcher, chosen by Phildelphia A's manager Connie Mack to open the 1929 World Series against the Cubs, who not only won the game but set a Series record with 13 strikeouts?
    a) Lefty Grove
    b) Grover Cleveland Alexander
    c) Howard Ehmke
    d) Goofy Gomez

30. Babe Ruth struck out 30 times in 129 World Series at-bats, but only one of the pitchers listed below ever struck him out with the bases loaded:
    a) Rosy Ryan
    b) Art Nehf
    c) Charley Root
    d) Grover Cleveland Alexander

31. What two brothers won all four games for the Cardinals in the 1934 World Series?

32. Who batted cleanup for the Boston Red Sox when they won the 1918 World Series and never played another major league game after that season?

33. Who is the only pitcher ever to hurl a no-hitter in World Series play, and what made that achievement so special?

34. What St. Louis Cardinals pitcher set a World Series strikeout record, how many and against which team?

L.	True or false: If a player is traded from one major league to another in midseason, his at-bats in both leagues do not count toward qualifying for the batting title.

35. Can you name the home plate umpire when Don Larsen tossed his perfect game in the 1956 World Series?

36. One of the World Series' most dramatic moments came in the 12th inning of the 1975 World Series with Carlton Fisk at bat. What happened?

37. What Cardinals catcher was MVP of the 1982 World Series?

38. The first World Series was played in 1903, the second in 1905. Who won the AL and NL pennants in 1904, and why didn't they play the World Series?

Answers

1. Carbo was pinch hitting for pitcher Roger Moret, and he hit a three-run homer that tied the score, 6-6, and set the stage for the Sox' dramatic 12th-inning victory.

2. Dale Mitchell of the Dodgers took a called third strike to end Don Larsen's perfect game.

3. Jose Santiago of the Red Sox (1967) and Mickey Lolich of the Tigers (1968) each hit HRs in their first Series at-bat.

4. Dave McNally of the Orioles hit a grand-slam homer against the Reds in the 1971 World Series.

5. Pittsburgh over Washington, 1925; New York Yankees over Milwaukee, 1958; Detroit over St. Louis Cards, 1968; Pittsburgh over Baltimore, 1979; Kansas City over St. Louis Cards, 1985

The California Angels played in this stadium for one season while their Angel Stadium was being constructed during the early sixties.

6. The New York Mets won the 1969 World Series by beating the Baltimore Orioles.

7. a) New York Yankees have been in 32 Series and won 22 times.

8. Cookie Lavagetto pinch hit for Eddie Stanky in the ninth inning and sliced a two-out, game-winning hit off the right field wall at Ebbets Field for a 3-2 victory.

9. Rick Wise, who pitched for the Red Sox in the 1975 World Series

10. The American League holds a 49-35 edge.

11. Bill Mazeroski hit a 10th-inning home run off the Yankees' Ralph Terry in the seventh game of the 1960 Series.

12. First baseman Dick Stuart, as a pinch-hitter

13. c) The 1979 Pittsburgh Pirates

14. Charley Root

15. Willie McCovey

16. Harry Walker got the hit, and Enos Slaughter scored all the way from first base.

17. True. Cobb hit .262 in World Series play.

18. b) Casey Stengel hit a solo homer for the New York Giants in the 1-0 win over the Yankees in 1923.

19. d) Grover Cleveland Alexander was 39 years, 7 months

when he beat the Yankees for the Cardinals in 1926.

20. Catcher Charley Silvera of the Yankees

21. Jim Thorpe played in the 1917 World Series for the New York Giants.

22. d) Sammy Byrd was an outfielder for the Yankees in 1932.

23. Mary Schoendienst, wife of Cardinals manager Red Schoendienst, did it prior to a game in the 1968 World Series.

24. Earle (Greasy) Neale led the Eagles to a pair of NFL titles and also played for the Cincinnati Reds in the 1919 World Series.

25. a) Christy Mathewson of the New York Giants had four World Series shutouts.

26. Lou Burdette

27. Tris Speaker, Bill Terry, Rogers Hornsby and Lou Boudreau

28. b) Frankie Frisch

29. c) Howard Ehmke

30. a) Rosy Ryan of the New York Giants struck out Ruth with the bases loaded in the eighth inning of the sixth game of the 1923 World Series.

31. Dizzy and Paul (Daffy) Dean

32. George Whiteman, a right-handed hitter, was in the

lineup because the Chicago Cubs started six left-handed pitchers.

33. Don Larsen beat the Dodgers in the 1956 Series by pitching a perfect-game no-hitter.

34. Bob Gibson of the St. Louis Cardinals struck out 17 Detroit Tigers in the opening game of the 1968 World Series.

35. Babe Pinelli

36. With the score tied, 6-6, Fisk led off the 12th inning of the sixth game and hit a solo home run over the left field wall at Fenway Park for a 7-6 Red Sox victory, tying the Series at three games apiece.

37. Darrell Porter

38. The New York Giants of the NL refused to play the AL champion Boston Pilgrims in the 1904 World Series.

Hitters/Sluggers

1. What player established a major league record for hitting one or more home runs in the most major league parks, and how many parks were his victims?

2. What player holds the major league record for the most pinch hits?

3. In 1950 the Red Sox had a .302 team batting average. Which of the players listed below won the league's batting title?
   Billy Goodman
   Johnny Pesky
   Dom DiMaggio
   Ted Williams

4. True or false: Babe Ruth hit three home runs for the Boston Braves in his final major league game.

5. Who is the former All-America wide receiver from Michigan State, a number-two pick of the St. Louis Football Cardinals, who became a home-run bashing outfielder for the Detroit Tigers and is now a Los Angeles Dodger?

6. True or False: Pete Rose and Mickey Mantle are the only switch-hitters ever to win batting titles.

M. True or false: At one time in major league baseball a pitcher could intentionally walk a hitter by throwing to third base four straight times while the batter stood in the batter's box.

7. True or false: Luke Appling never batted over .400 during a major league season.

8. What American League player holds the record for the best season's batting average?

9. Who are the only National League players since 1901 to bat over .400 for a single season?

10. Who holds the record for the highest batting average for a single major league season?
    a) Ted Williams
    b) Ty Cobb
    c) George Sisler
    d) Rogers Hornsby

11. Who was the last National League player to hit over .400 for one season?

12. Who was the first player ever to hit more than 50 home runs in one season?

This famous football stadium was the site of the 1959 World Series and the scene of the greatest crowd in Series history.

13. What was the major difference between the season home-run records set by Babe Ruth and Roger Maris, one that placed an asterisk beside Maris's name?

N. After hitting a home run, the batter snaps his Achilles' tendon while rounding second base and cannot continue his trip to home plate. A pinch runner finishes the trip, but who gets credit for the hit and for the run scored?

14. Babe Ruth established the home-run record of 60, and it took Roger Maris 34 years to break it, but still the players had what three things in common?

15. Willie Mays and Johnny Mize each hit 51 home runs in one season, and though they did it eight years apart, what was the one thing their feat had in common?

16. Can you name the American League players who, eight times in league history, hit more than 50 homers in one season?

17. Who is the former Cubs player who holds both the NL record for home runs and the major league record for RBIs in one season, and when did he do it?

18. Which of the players listed below are the only National Leaguers ever to hit more than 50 home runs twice in their careers?
    Willie McCovey
    Frank Robinson
    Ralph Kiner
    Willie Mays
    George Foster
    Darryl Strawberry

19. Can you name the NL hitters who slugged 50 or more homers in a single season?

20. Stan Musial is the National League's number-two all-time hitter with 3,630. Can you break down the number he got at home and on the road?

O.	A batting helmet is lying in foul territory when a batted ball strikes it, and ricochets fair. Can the runner beat out a hit to first base in this circumstance?

21. Six times in major league history a batter has hit 56 or more homers in a single season. Can you name the hitters, their numbers and the years?

22. Whose record did Babe Ruth break when he hit 60 home runs in 1927?

23. Against what team and what pitcher did Roger Maris hit his record-setting 61st home run in 1961?

24. Within ten, how many at-bats did Babe Ruth have in 1927 when he hit 60 homers, and how many did Roger Maris have in 1961 when he hit 61 home runs?

25. Can you name the hitters who have had seasons of 30 or more homers in both major leagues?

26. Which American League third baseman has hit the most lifetime home runs?
    a) Brooks Robinson
    b) Graig Nettles
    c) Buddy Bell
    d) George Brett

27. True or false: The Kansas City A's had no 20-game winners during the decade of the sixties.

P. With a runner on second, none out and an 0-2 count on the batter, the runner breaks for third base. The pitch to the batter bounces in the dirt *en route* to the plate, ticks off the hitter's bat and into the catcher's glove. He then throws to third base to nail the runner. Foul ball or double play?

28. What pitcher gave up Babe Ruth's final American League home run?

29. Who were the last players to hit more home runs by themselves than an entire team in the same season?

30. True or false: Babe Ruth twice hit more home runs in one season than any other team in the American League during the same season.

31. True or false: Roger Maris was not walked intentionally during the 1961 season when he hit his 61 homers.

32. What three players finished within seven-tenths of each other in the battle for the 1931 National League batting title?

33. Which hitter holds the major league record for hitting three or more home runs in a single game?

34. True or false: Ty Cobb hit more career home runs than Pete Rose.

Q. What is the formula by which a pitcher's earned run average is figured?

35. Which National League hitters hold the consecutive game hitting streak?

36. Pete Rose became baseball's all-time hit-maker when he passed Ty Cobb in 1985, but who ranks number three?

37. Who was the American League batting champion whose father once rode the second-place finisher in a Kentucky Derby?

38. Pitchers being cautious with a dangerous hitter is one thing, but which player was the first in the AL to walk six times in a nine-inning game?
    a) Jimmie Foxx
    b) Lou Gehrig
    c) Babe Ruth
    d) Mickey Mantle

39. Which of these players holds the record for hitting the most home runs in one park?
    Mel Ott
    Babe Ruth
    Ted Williams
    Hank Aaron

40. Who holds the major league record among catchers for hitting the most career home runs?

41. Batting around is one thing, but who was the first American League hitter to bat three times in the same inning?

R. On a play at the plate, the umpire rules the runner safe and the catcher begins a bitter protest while the hitter continues around third and also slides in during the argument. Is that second run allowed?

42. Who is the only American League player to hit 400 home runs among more than 3,000 base hits?

43. Ted Williams was the last major league hitter to bat over .400 for a season, but can you recount his average on the final day of that 1941 season, and what he did that day to achieve that feat?

44. Henry Aaron retruned to Milwaukee, where he began his major league career, to play his final two seasons with the Brewers after that AL club sent which two players to Atlanta in the deal?

45. Who is the only major league hitter ever to drive in 12 runs in one game?

46. When Stan Musial established an NL hit record of 3,160 in 1960, whose record did he break?

47. Fours were wild the night that Henry Aaron broke Babe Ruth's career home-run mark of 714. How many fours were involved?

48. One of Ted Williams's many major league records is reaching base how many consecutive times?

S.	The bases are loaded with two out, and the batter hits a home run over the fence. All the baserunners stop to watch the towering drive while the batter, ecstatic at his feat, doesn't notice the runner on first hasn't moved, and passes him. How many runs are allowed to score?

49. Tony Gwynn, the NL's top hitter in 1987, was the first player in San Diego history ever to be drafted by two teams from that city. Who are they?

50. Who is the only player in National League history to hit more than 55 home runs in a single season?
   a) Hack Wilson
   b) Hank Aaron
   c) George Foster
   d) Willie Mays

51. True or false: Babe Ruth hit 50 or more home runs in eight different major league seasons.

52. Who is the all-time pinch-hit home-run leader?

53. Who were the pitchers who
   a) served up Pete Rose's final hit for an all-time record of 4,204; and
   b) who faced him in his last at-bat?

54. These Hall-of-Fame outfield brothers who played for the Pirates were known as Big Poison and Little Poison. Who were they?

55. What was the count on Henry Aaron when he hit his 715th career home run, breaking Babe Ruth's record?

T. Two outs, bases loaded, and the batter walks, but ball four sails past the catcher. Runner from second rounds the third base but, seeing the catcher retrieve the ball, tries to get back and is thrown out before the original runner on third can touch home plate from the walk. When he does, will the run count?

56. Match these famous hitters with their nicknames:

Babe Ruth	Rajah
Joe DiMaggio	Flying Scot
Ted Williams	The Kid
Bobby Thomson	Yaz
Willie Mays	Yankee Clipper
Stan Musial	The Bambino
Rogers Hornsby	Splendid Splinter
Carl Yastrzemski	The Man

57. Against what pitcher, what team, what game and on what pitch did Henry Aaron tie Babe Ruth's record of 714 home runs?

58. Which of the listed players won the major league batting title in their first full season?

Tony Oliva, Twins, 1964	Don Mattingly, Yanks, 1984
Pete Rose, Reds, 1962	Peter Reiser, Dodgers, 1941
Lefty O'Doul, Phils, 1929	Ty Cobb, Tigers, 1907
Wade Boggs, Red Sox, 1983	Ted Williams, Red Sox, 1939
Benny Kauff, Indians, 1914	Del Ennis, Phils, 1947

59. Which Yankee player hit the most inside-the-park home runs during his career?

60. Which of the players listed below had 200 hits in a season four or more times?

Ted Williams	Joe Medwick
Stan Musial	Tris Speaker
Pete Rose	Joe DiMaggio
Lou Gehrig	Rod Carew

61. How many times has Wade Boggs of the Red Sox won the American League batting title during the decade of the eighties?

62. Name the two National League players who have won a pair of batting titles during the eighties.

U. In a 1959 game, Harvey Haddix of the Pirates hadn't allowed any Milwaukee Braves to reach base until the 13th inning, when an error and an intentional walk allowed Felix Mantilla and Hank Aaron to reach base. The next hitter, Joe Adcock, hit a ball over the right field wall. Aaron, seeing Mantilla score, broke off his path around the bases, and went to the dugout. Adcock continued, thinking the ball was a home run. Was it?

63. Can you match the year and the American League batting champion:

1980	Wade Boggs
1981	Don Mattingly
1982	George Brett
1983	Carney Lansford
1984	Willie Wilson

64. Can you match the year and the National League batting champion:

1980	Bill Madlock
1981	Willie McGee
1982	Tim Raines
1984	Bill Buckner
1985	Al Oliver
1986	Tony Gwynn

65. How many National League home run titles has Mike Schmidt of the Phillies won or shared during the eighties?

66. Can you match the year and the player who won a National League home run title during the eighties:

1980	Dave Kingman
1982	Mike Schmidt
1985	Dale Murphy
1987	Andre Dawson

67. Match the year and the American League home run champion:

1983	Darrell Evans
1984	Mark McGwire
1985	Jim Rice
1986	Jesse Barfield
1987	Tony Armas

68. How many RBI titles has Mike Schmidt of the Phillies won or shared during the eighties?

69. Can you match the year with the player who won the American League's RBI title:

1980	Joe Carter
1981	Don Mattingly
1982	Eddie Murray
1984	Cecil Cooper
1985	George Bell
1986	Tony Armas
1987	Hal McRae

V. A runner on first; the batter hits a ball to the shortstop, who bobbles it but manages to tag second base with his glove while holding the ball in his bare hand. Safe or out?

70. How many home runs, within five, did Hall-of-Famer Willie

Stargell hit during the seventies, to lead the majors in that department?

71. What Hall-of-Famer won the Triple Crown for Cincinnati in 1966?

72. What two players, who between them hit 1,341 home runs during their major league careers, were inducted into the Hall of Fame in 1982?

Answers

1. Frank Robinson hit home runs in 32 different parks.

2. a) Manny Mota

3. a) Billy Goodman won the AL batting title in 1950 with a .354 mark.

4. False. Ruth hit his last three home runs in a game for the Braves against the Pirates on May 25, 1935, but he played his final major league game on May 30, 1935, when the Braves met the Phillies.

5. Kirk Gibson

6. True

7. True

The Cleveland Indians used this park before moving full-time into their current Lakefront Stadium over a half century ago.

8. Nap Lajoie of the Philadelphia A's hit .422 in 1901.

9. Rogers Hornsby and Bill Terry

10. d) Rogers Hornsby of the Cardinals hit .424 in 1924.

11. Bill Terry batted .401 in 1930.

12. d) Ruth hit 54 in 1970.

13. Ruth hit his during a 154-game season (actually in 155 games), while Maris's was accomplished during a 162-game season.

14. Both were left-handed hitters; both played in Yankee Stadium as members of the Yankees; and both were rightfielders.

15. Both played for the New York Giants in the Polo Grounds.

16. Babe Ruth did it four times; Jimmie Foxx, Hank Greenberg, Mickey Mantle and Roger Maris.

17. Hack Wilson hit 56 home runs in 1930, the same season he also drove in 190 runs for the Cubs.

18. Ralph Kiner (1947, 1949), and Willie Mays (1955, 1965)

19. Hack Wilson of the Cubs hit 56 in 1930; Raplh Kiner did it twice, 54 in 1949, and he tied Johnny Mize with 51 in 1947; Willie Mays also did it twice, 52 in 1965 and 51 in 1955; and George Foster hit 52 in 1977.

20. Musial had 1,815 hits at home, and 1,815 hits on the road during his career.

21. Roger Maris hit 61 in 1961; Jimmie Foxx (1932) and Hank Greenberg (1938) each hit 58; Hack Wilson of the Cubs (1930) hit 56; and Babe Ruth did it twice, 1921 (59) and 1927 (60).

22. His own. He hit 59 in 1921.

23. Maris's record-setting homer came against the Red Sox's Tracy Stallard.

24. Ruth hit his 60 homers in 540 at-bats, and Maris got his in 590.

25. Frank Robinson (Reds, NL; Orioles, Angels, AL); Frank Howard (Dodgers, NL; Senators, AL); Dick Stuart (Pirates, NL; Red Sox, AL); Rich Allen (Phils, Cards, NL; White Sox, AL); Bobby Bonds (Giants, NL; Yankees, Angels, White Sox, Rangers, AL); Reggie Smith (Red Sox, AL; Dodgers, NL); and Jeff Boroughs (Rangers, AL; Braves, NL)

26. b) Graig Nettles, who played with both the Indians and Yankees

27. True

28. Sid Cohen of the Washington Senators on September 29, 1934

29. Joe DiMaggio of the Yankees and Ken Keltner of the Indians hit 39 and 32, respectively, in 1948, while the entire Washington Senators team that season hit only 31.

30. True, with his 54 in 1920 and 60 in 1927

31. True

32. Chic Hafey won the NL batting title with a .3489 average; Bill Terry of the Giants was second with .3486; and Jim Bottomley of the Cards was third with .3482.

33. d) Johnny Mize did it six times.

34. False. Cobb had 118, Rose 160.

35. Wee Willie Keeler (1897) and Pete Rose (1978) each hit safely in 44 straight games.

36. Hank Aaron, with 3,771 hits

37. Ferris Fain of the 1951–52 Philadelphia A's won the batting title. His father, Oscar, rode the second-place finisher in the 1912 Derby.

38. Jimmie Foxx of the Red Sox, on June 16, 1938

39. a) Mel Ott hit 323 home runs in the Polo Grounds.

40. b) Johnny Bench

41. d) Ted Williams, in the seventh inning on July 4, 1948

42. b) Carl Yastrzemski

43. Williams went into that final day batting .399 and went 6-for-8 in a doubleheader to finish with .406.

44. The Brewers traded outfielder Dave May and pitcher Roger Alexander to Atlanta for Aaron on November 2, 1974.

45. Jim Bottomley of the Cardinals did it in 1924 against the Brooklyn Dodgers, with a grand slam, a two-run homer,

two two-run singles, a one-run double and a run-scoring single.

46. Musial broke the 45-year-old record of Honus Wagner. He later went on to set his own record of 3,630.

47. Aaron and Dodgers pitcher Al Downing each wore uniform number 44; Aaron hit his record-smashing home run in the fourth inning of a game played in the fourth month in a year ending in four (1974) where he was the fourth hitter in the Braves' lineup.

48. Williams reached base 16 consecutive times during the 1957 season with two singles, four homers, nine walks and once being hit by a pitch.

49. Gwynn was drafted by the San Diego Padres and the NBA's San Diego Clippers in 1981.

50. a) Hack Wilson of the Cubs hit 56 in 1930.

51. False. He did it four times.

52. Cliff Johnson, who played with a number of teams in the seventies and eighties, is the all-time leader with 19.

53. Greg Minton of the Giants gave up Rose's final major league hit, a single, on August 14, 1986; Goose Gossage of the Padres struck him out on three pitches in his final at-bat.

54. Paul (Big Poison) and Lloyd (Little Poison) Waner

55. Aaron had a 1-1 count from pitcher Al Downing.

56. Rajah—Rogers Hornsby; Flying Scot—Bobby Thom-

son; The Kid—Willie Mays; Yaz—Carl Yastrzemski; Yankee Clipper—Joe DiMaggio; The Bambino—Babe Ruth; Splendid Splinter—Ted Williams; The Man—Stan Musial

57. Aaron tied Ruth's record by hitting the first pitch of the first game he played in 1982 from Cincinnati pitcher Jack Billingham.

58. Oliva, O'Doul, Boggs, Kauff, Mattingly, Reiser and Cobb

59. Mickey Mantle, with five

60. Rose, Gehrig, Medwick, Speaker and Carew

61. Boggs has won four batting titles during the 80s—1983, 1985, 1986 and 1987.

62. Bill Madlock of Pittsburgh (1981 and 1983) and Tony Gwynn of the Padres (1984 and 1987)

63. 1980—Brett; 1981—Lansford; 1982—Wilson; 1983—Boggs; 1984—Mattingly

64. 1980—Buckner; 1981—Madlock; 1982—Oliver; 1984—Gwynn; 1985—McGee; 1986—Raines

65. Schmidt has won or shared five titles.

66. 1980—Schmidt; 1982—Kingman; 1985—Murphy; 1987—Dawson

67. 1983—Rice; 1984—Armas; 1985—Evans; 1986—Barfield; 1987—McGwire

68. Schmidt has won or shared the NL RBI title four times during the eighties (1980 through 1986).

69. 1980—Cooper; 1981—Murray; 1982—McRae; 1984—Armas; 1985—Mattingly; 1986—Carter; 1987—Bell

70. Stargell hit 296 homers during the seventies.

71. Frank Robinson

72. Henry Aaron and Frank Robinson

This stadium was where Mickey Mantle hit his famous "tape measure" home run that traveled over 500 feet.

Pitchers

1. Who is the LA Dodgers' left-handed pitcher who made a big splash as a rookie when, in ten late-season relief appearances in 1980, he didn't allow a run?

2. What is the record for the most hits allowed by a major league pitcher in a shutout?

3. What Hall-of-Fame pitcher once toured with the Harlem Globetrotters?

4. In 1938 pitcher Johnny Vander Meer of the Reds achieved what never-happened-before-or-since feat?

5. Which pitcher recorded the most one-hitters during his career?
   a) Nolan Ryan
   b) Sandy Koufax
   c) Bob Feller
   d) Grover Cleveland Alexander

6. Can you name the pitchers and teams who exchanged back-to-back no-hitters during the 1968 season?

W.	Can a pitcher stay in the game at a different position after a second visit to the mound by his manager?

7. What pitcher holds the modern-day record for most consecutive victories?

8. True or false: Nolan Ryan once won 20 games for a last-place team.

9. Who holds the National League record for starting the most games in one season?
   a) Phil Niekro
   b) Sandy Koufax
   c) Steve Carlton
   d) Tom Seaver

10. Who holds the American League record for starting the most games in a single season?

11. What pitcher hit the most home runs in major league history?

12. Who was the only relief pitcher ever to win the MVP award?

13. Who was the first relief pitcher ever to win the Cy Young award?
   a) Tug McGraw
   b) Make Marshall
   c) Goose Gossage
   d) Jeff Reardon

X.	With a runner on third and one out, the batter hits a long fly to the outfield that can be caught. The runner moves up to the left field line, above third base, and then times his run toward the plate to touch third base just as the ball is caught. Legal?

14. Who was the first American League relief pitcher to win the Cy Young award?

15. What major league pitcher started only 52 of his 1,070 games?

16. Can you name the pitchers from among those listed below who have pitched no-hitters in their first major league game?

Sandy Koufax	Robin Roberts
Addie Joss	Walter Johnson
Juan Marichal	Mike Fornieles
Dick Fowler	Bill Lee

17. What great relief pitcher helped the Yankees to a pair of world championships in the late forties?

18. What major league relief pitcher hit a home run in his first at-bat?
    a) Sparky Lyle
    b) Dick Radatz
    c) Hoyt Wilhelm
    d) Tim Lollar

19. What Cleveland Indians pitcher beat the Red Sox in a one-game playoff in 1948 for the American League championship?

20. True or false: old time pitcher Mordecai (Three-fingered) Brown really pitched with just three fingers on his right

hand.

Y. A runner goes from first to third on a single, but the defense wants an appeal play, believing the runner didn't tag second base. The pitcher backs off the rubber and tosses toward second base, but the runner on third breaks for home. The shortstop cuts off the pitcher's soft toss and throws home, too late, to get the runner. Can there be a re-appeal that negates the run?

21. True or false: Ted Williams pitched for the Red Sox.

22. Who was Steve Carlton's constant batterymate in St. Louis and Philadelphia who once cracked: "When we die, we'll both be buried 60 feet, 6 inches from each other"?

23. Who is the only pitcher ever to lose a regulation nine-inning-game no-hitter?

24. True or false: Babe Ruth's final major league pitching appearance was in 1933.

25. What is the major league record for the most home runs allowed by one team's pitching staff in a season?

26. Which player listed below was the 3,000th strikeout victim of both Bob Gibson (1974) and Nolan Ryan (1980)?
    a) Pete Rose
    b) Tony Perez
    c) Cesar Geronimo
    d) Lou Brock

27. What three Cy Young award winners were teammates on the Orioles' pitching staff during the early eighties?

Z.	During a game, a pitcher is used as a pinch-runner for the designated hitter and then stays in the game to pitch. Can his team insert a DH to hit for him and still allow him to pitch?

28. On their birth certificates, the Dean Brothers were named Jay and Paul, but in major league baseball they were known as:
    a) Frick and Frack
    b) Goofy and Mickey
    c) Romeo and Juliet
    d) Dizzy and Daffy

29. What pitcher had eight 20-win seasons in the major leagues, yet still holds the single-season record for most losses?
    a) Tom Seaver
    b) Walter Johnson
    c) Gaylord Perry
    d) Vic Willis

30. Who was the first left-handed pitcher in the major leagues to reach 3,000 strikeouts?
    a) Sandy Koufax
    b) Hal Newhouser
    c) Steve Carlton
    d) Nolan Ryan

31. Who was the oldest pitcher ever to start a game in the major leagues?
    a) Satchel Paige
    b) Hoyt Wilhelm
    c) Jim Perry
    d) Phil Niekro

32. Long gone is the feat of pitching both ends of a doubleheader (long gone is the doubleheader!). Who is the pitcher who earned a nickname for that feat, and what did he accomplish?

33. Who was the famous slugger who was once involved as a pitcher in a perfect game?

34. Match the five pitchers from the list on the left with the teams against whom they pitched perfect games, since 1960.

Sandy Koufax	Mets
Mike Witt	Cubs
Steve Carlton	Twins
Jim Bunning	Blue Jays
Fernando Valenzuela	Rangers
Catfish Hunter	
Jim Palmer	
Len Barker	

AA. Runners on second and third, none out. The batter hits a sacrifice fly to the center, scoring the man from third. The runner at second attempts to reach third and is thrown out. Does the batter get credit for a sacrifice fly even though he has hit into a double play?

35. What pitcher once pitched 12 innings of perfect baseball, getting credit for one of the majors' perfect games, yet lost the game in the 13th inning?

36. What two pitchers halted Pete Rose's NL-record 44-game hitting streak, and which of them got him the final time?

37. What hitter finally broke Johnny Vander Meer's hitless string after he had hurled two straight no-hitters in 1938?

38. For nearly a quarter century, (1921–1943), the New York Yankees were managed by Miller Huggins and Joe McCarthy, two of the greatest in the game's history, with the exception of one season by which man?

39. Match the pitchers with their nicknames:

Sal Maglie	Mad Hungarian
Fernando Valenzuela	Springfield Rifle
Vernon Gomez	The Barber
Bill Lee	The Toothpick
Al Hrbobsky	Spaceman
Sam Jones	El Toro
Vic Raschi	Goofy

40. Match the year and the pitcher who won the American League's Cy Young award:

1980	Bret Saberhagen
1981	Willie Hernandez
1982	Roger Clemens
1983	Steve Stone
1984	LaMarr Hoyt
1985	Rollie Fingers
1986	Pete Vuckovich

41. What pitcher has won the most Cy Young awards?

BB. How would you score this play? A batter hits a long drive to centerfield, and as he rounds second base en route to third he trips over the feet of the shortstop, whose only intention was to receive the throw from the cutoff man. The runner stays at second until the umpire directs him to take third base because of interference. Is it a double and third base given on interference, or is it scored as a triple?

42. Match the year and the National League pitchers who won

Two major league teams, one of them the forerunners of the Baltimore Orioles, shared this park for half a century.

the Cy Young award:

1980	Fernando Valenzuela
1981	Rick Sutcliffe
1983	Steve Carlton
1984	Steve Bedrosian
1985	John Denny
1986	Mike Scott
1987	Dwight Gooden

43. Name the two pitchers who each have won three strikeout titles, in the National and American Leagues respectively, during the eighties.

CC. Runners on first and second, none out, when the batter pops up between the pitcher and catcher. The umpire calls "infield fly," but the catcher and pitcher collide going for the ball, and it hits the ground, untouched, and spins into foul territory. What is the call?

Answers

1. Ferando Valenzuela, who had never pitched in the majors until that late-season call-up

2. Larry Cheyney of the Cubs and Milt Gaston of the Senators share the mark of 14 hits in hurling shutouts.

3. Bob Gibson, who pitched for the St. Louis Cardinals and was a basketball star at Creighton University

4. Vander Meer pitched back-to-back no-hitters, against Boston on June 11, and Brooklyn on June 15.

5. c) Bob Feller of the Indians had 12.

6. Ray Washburn of the Cardinals no-hit the Giants on September 18, 1968, the day after Gaylord Perry of the Giants had no-hit the Cardinals.

7. In 1912 Rube Marquard of the New York Giants won his first 19 games.

8. True—22 for the last-place California Angels in 1974

9. a) Phil Niekro holds the NL record for most starts in one season with 44 in 1979.

10. d) Wilbur Wood started a record 49 games for the Chicago White Sox in 1972.

11. Wes Ferrell hit 38 home runs during his major league pitching career.

12. Jim Konstanty of the 1950 Phillies

13. b) Mike Marshall of the Dodgers, in 1974

14. Sparky Lyle of the Yankees, in 1977

15. Hoyt Wilhelm

16. Joss (Cleveland), Marichal (Giants) and Fornieles (Washington)

17. Joe Page

18. c) Hoyt Wilhelm of the New York Giants

19. Gene Bearden

20. False. He really had four after an accident as a youth

badly mauled his hand. It didn't stop him from winning 208 games in the major leagues, however, and being elected to the Hall of Fame.

21. True. In 1940 he pitched the last two innings of a game against Detroit, allowed three hits, walked none and struck out one batter.

22. Catcher Tim McCarver

23. Ken Johnson of the Astros lost to the Reds, 1-0, in 1964. Eight other pitchers have lost no-hitters in extra innings.

24. True. Ruth pitched a 6-5, complete-game victory for the Yankees on the final game of the season, beating Washington.

25. The pitchers of the 1964 Kansas City A's allowed 220 homers, tops for a 162-game season. The Kansas City A's staff of 1956 allowed 187, the record for a 154-game schedule.

26. c) Cesar Geronimo

27. Jim Palmer, Mike Flanagan and Steve Stone

28. d) Jay (Dizzy) and Paul (Daffy) Dean

29. d) Vic Willis, who won 244 games in the NL, lost 29 of the Boston Braves' 103 losses in 1905.

30. c) Steve Carlton, pitching for the Phillies, achieved the mark on April 29, 1981, against Montreal. Ryan achieved it in 1980, but he is right-handed.

31. c) Satchel Paige was 60 years old when he started a game

for the Kansas City A's against the Red Sox in 1965, pitching three innings and leaving with a 1-0 lead. The A's eventually lost the game.

32. Joseph (Ironman) McGinty of the New York Giants won three doubleheaders as a starting pitcher in 1903, and five during his major league career.

33. Babe Ruth, when pitching for the Red Sox, started the first game of a doubleheader on June 23, 1917, and after walking the game's leadoff batter, he was tossed out of the game for squawking on the play. Manager Jack Barry brought in Ernie Shore. On his first pitch, the runner, Ray Morgan, was thrown out trying to steal. Shore got the next 26 batters and was given credit for a perfect game.

34. Bunnings beat the Mets, Koufax beat the Cubs, Hunter beat the Twins, Barker beat the Blue Jays and Witt beat the Rangers.

35. Harvey Haddix of the Pirates pitched 12 perfect innings against the Braves in 1959, but lost the game in the 13th on an error, sacrifice, intentional walk and the only hit he surrendered—a double. Still, he is given credit for a 12-inning perfect game.

36. Larry McWilliams started for the Braves and got Rose the first three times, and Gene Garber ended the streak by striking him out.

37. Deb Garms of the Braves singled to left centerfield with one out in the fourth inning, June 19, 1938.

38. Bob Shawkey managed the club in 1930 after Huggins's death, and was replaced in 1931 by McCarthy.

39. Mad Hungarian—Al Hrbobsky; Springfield Rifle—Vic Raschi; The Barber—Sal Maglie; The Toothpick—Sam Jones; Spaceman—Bill Lee; El Toro—Fernando Valenzuela; Goofy—Vernon Gomez

40. 1980—Stone; 1981—Fingers; 1982—Vuckovich; 1983—Hoyt; 1984—Hernandez; 1985—Saberhagen; 1986—Clemens

41. Steve Carlton is the Cy Young award leader with four.

42. 1980—Carlton; 1981—Valenzuela; 1983—Denny; 1984—Sutcliffe; 1985—Gooden; 1986—Scott; 1987—Bedrosian

43. Steve Carlton of the Phils (1980-82-83) and Mark Langston of Seattle (1984-86-87)

All-Star Game

1. Who is the only pitcher ever to give up three home runs in an All-Star Game?

2. Who is the youngest player ever to appear in an All Star Game, Robin Yount of Milwaukee or Butch Wynegar of the Twins?

3. Who is the only pitcher to start an All-Star Game for both leagues?

4. Who was the first player to play for both leagues in an All-Star Game?
   a) Schoolboy Rowe
   b) Catfish Hunter
   c) Marvelous Marv Throneberry
   d) Toothpick Sam Jones

5. Which manager has lost the most All-Star Games?
   a) Sparky Anderson
   b) Walter Alston
   c) Casey Stengel
   d) Billy Martin

6. What family has had the most members appear in an All-Star Game?
   a) The Bradys
   b) The DiMaggios
   c) The Perrys
   d) The Trapps

DD.	A batter is hit by a pitch, but not disabled. Still he goes directly to the dugout and is replaced by a runner at first place. When time is back in, the pitcher assumes a stance, steps off the runner and throws to first base for an appeal. Safe or out?

7. How many grand-slam homers have been hit in the All-Star Game?

8. Who was the first player to get four hits in an All-Star Game?
   a) Joe Medwick, 1937
   b) Lou Gehrig, 1935
   c) Joe DiMaggio, 1936
   d) Ted Williams, 1941

9. Who holds the career record for striking out in an All-Star Game?

10. True or false: Outfielder Richie Ashburn was the first New York Mets player to play in an All-Star Game.

11. Who were the last two players to represent the St. Louis

Browns in an All-Star Game?
a) Pitchers Nelson Garvey and Billy Potter, 1948
b) Shortstop Junior Stephens and outfielder Pete Gray, 1946
c) Shortstop Billy Hunter and pitcher Satchel Paige, 1953
d) Infielder Eddie Gaedell and catcher Max Patkin, 1947

12. What year was the first All-Star Game played at night, and what was the site?

13. Who committed the only error in the very first All-Star Game in 1933?

EE. With a runner on third and none out, the batter hits a towering drive to the outfield which the baserunner believes will be a home run, and he races across the plate before seeing the centerfielder has an opportunity to catch the ball. He retraces his steps, touching home en route back to third, but as he hits the bag, the fielder drops the ball. The runner immediately heads for the plate again, but is thrown out. Or is he?

14. Who was the first player to hit two home runs in one All-Star Game?

15. Who was the only player who got a hit in the 1934 All-Star Game who was not elected to the Hall of Fame?

16. Who was the famed sports editor of the *Chicago Tribune* who originated the All-Star Game, in both baseball and football, as well as creating the old All-America Football Conference?

17. Who is the only player ever to steal home in an All-Star

Game?
a) Pie Traynor, 1934
b) George Case, 1939
c) Bobby Doerr, 1942
d) Pete Reiser, 1943

18. Who has hit the most home runs in All-Star competition?
a) Ted Williams
b) Mike Schmidt
c) Reggie Jackson
d) Stan Musial

19. Was Mickey Mantle or Willie Mays the only player ever to hit a home run and steal a base in the same All-Star Game?

20. Who are the only two players ever to make unassisted double plays in an All-Star Game?

FF. True or false: A team can move one of its fielders behind the catcher to back him up in case of a wild pitch.

21. Who were the first black players to appear in an All-Star Game?

22. When and at what site was the first All-Star Game played on the West Coast?

23. Which manager has won the most All-Star Games?
a) Walter Alston
b) Casey Stengel
c) Sparky Anderson
d) Joe McCarthy

24. In the 1934 All-Star Game, starting AL pitcher Carl Hubbell gave up a leadoff single to Charley Gehringer and walked

Heinie Manush. Then he had to face, in order, Babe Ruth, Lou Gehrig, Jimmie Foxx, Al Simmons and Joe Cronin, who between them accumulated over 2,000 career home runs and were all Hall-of-Famers. What happened?

25. In the 1941 game at Detroit, the AL All-Stars trailed, 5-4, with two out, two runners on base in the ninth inning, and Ted Williams at bat. What happened?

26. How many positions has Pete Rose started during his All-Star Game appearances?

GG. With a runner on first base, the batter grounds a ball to the first baseman, who steps on the bag and then throws to second base to try and get the base runner. However, the runner, seeing the easy out, retreats toward first base after the out, and makes it back before the return throw. Is he safe or out?

Answers

1. b) Jim Palmer gave up three HRs in the 1977 All-Star Game.

2. Butch Wynegar of the Twins, who was 20 in 1976

3. d) Vida Blue

4. a) Schoolboy Rowe, as a pitcher from Detroit (1936) and the Philadelphia Phillies (1947)

5. c) Casey Stengel managed six losing All-Star teams.

6. b) The DiMaggios—Joe, Dom and Vince

7. One, by Fred Lynn of the AL in 1983

8. a) Joe Medwick of the Cardinals in 1937

9. a) Mickey Mantle, with 17 strikeouts

10. True, in the second All-Star Game of the 1962 season

11. c) Billy Hunter and Satchell Paige were the last Browns players to be named to an All-Star team.

12. a) 1943 at Shibe Park, Philadelphia

13. First baseman Lou Gehrig of the Yankees, playing for the American League

14. c) Arky Vaughn of the Pirates in 1941

15. Ben Chapman of the Yankees

16. Arch Ward

17. a) Pie Traynor of the Pirates, in 1934, stole the first base in an All-Star Game.

18. d) Stan Musial hit six home runs in All-Star play, most by any single player.

19. Willie Mays did it in the second All-Star Game in 1960.

20. First baseman Pete Runnels in the second All-Star Game in 1950, and first baseman Lee May of the Astros in 1972

21. In 1949, Jackie Robinson, Don Newcombe and Roy Campanella of the Dodgers, and Larry Doby of the Cleveland Indians were the first black players to appear in an All-Star Game.

22. The second All-Star Game in 1959 was played at the Los Angeles Coliseum, home of the Dodgers at that time.

23. a) Walter Alston won 7 All-Star Games as a manager.

24. Over two innings, Hubbell struck them out in succession.

25. Williams hit a titanic home run onto the roof at then Briggs Stadium to give the AL a dramatic 7-5 victory.

26. Rose started at four—right and left field, second and third base.

Base-Stealers

1. Which of the following players achieved his 50th stolen base in a single season in the fewest number of games?
   a) Maury Wills
   b) Rickey Henderson
   c) Tim Raines
   d) Lou Brock

2. Gus Triandos holds the major league record of going 1,206 games without ever being caught stealing. But there is a hooker in that record. What is it?
   a) He had such blazing speed, no one could nail him.
   b) He only tried to steal third base
   c) He never tried to steal a base after his only successful try with his very first game.
   d) He stole only one base in his entire career.

3. Maury Wills of the Dodgers led the National League six times in stolen bases, but how many times did he lead the

Bill Mazeroski hit a famous extra-inning home run over the left field wall of this park to win the 1960 World Series.

league in getting caught?

4. This great base-stealer also holds the record for being caught the most times attempting to steal. Who is he?

5. Two of the players listed below are the all-time leaders in their respective leagues for steals of home. Name them.

Amos Otis	Max Carey
Pete Reiser	George Case
Ty Cobb	Lou Brock
Rod Carew	Maury Wills

6. True or false: Rod Carew of the Twins was the last American League player to steal home seven times in one season.

HH. At the start of a game, the second player in the batting order mistakenly leads off and singles. Then the leadoff hitter steps to the plate, and with a 1-0 count, the opposition appeals the out-of-order routine. What is the ruling?

7. True or false: No one has stolen home twice in one major league game since 1958.

8. Did Lou Brock or Maury Wills lead the National League by stealing 50 or more bases in 12 different seasons?

9. Which of the players listed below led their respective leagues the most times in stolen bases:
   Max Carey
   Lou Brock
   Ty Cobb
   Maury Wills
   George Case
   Rickey Henderson
   Luis Aparicio
   Tim Raines

10. True or false: Rickey Henderson, then with the A's, holds the rookie record for most stolen bases.

11. Pick out the American and National League record-holders for consecutive stolen bases without being caught.

12. This player is the all-time major league career stolen base king with 938:
   a) Ty Cobb
   b) Maury Wills
   c) Rickey Henderson
   d) Lou Brock

13. Who holds the National League record for most stolen bases in one season, how many and what year?

II.	Bases loaded, two out, bottom of the ninth and the batter, with a 2-0 count, injures himself swinging at the third pitch severely enough to be replaced by a pinch-hitter. That batter then gets two more balls, for a walk-scoring run. Is either batter credited with an at-bat, and who gets the winning RBI?

14. Who holds the all-time season record for stolen bases and how many did he steal?

15. Who holds the season record for getting caught attempting to steal?

16. On June 15, 1964, the Cubs obtained pitchers Bobby Shantz, Ernie Broglio and Doug Clemens from the Cardinals for pitchers Jack Spring and Paul Toth and what outfielder who would become baseball's all-time base stealer with how many thefts?

17. Which American League player finally broke the season stolen base mark of 96 set by Ty Cobb in 1915?

18. Match these famous base-stealers with their nicknames:

Honus Wagner	Pepper
Tyrus Cobb	Flying Dutchman
George Sternweiss	Minnie
Peter Reiser	Ty
Orestes Minoso	Fordham Flash
George Martin	Snuffy
Frank Frisch	Pistol Pete

19. Can you name the two National League players who each have won three stolen base crowns during the eighties?

20. Name the only player other than Rickey Henderson to win an American League stolen base title during the eighties.
    a) Gary Pettis
    b) Don Baylor
    c) Harold Reynolds
    d) Julio Cruz

JJ. With runners on first and second, the batter hits a home run. While rounding the bases, the runner from first passes the runner on second, but quickly realizes his error, and retreats to the proper order. What is the call?

Answers

1. b) Rickey Henderson got his 50th stolen base in just his 51st 1982 game.

2. d) Triandos played from August 3, 1953, until August 15, 1965, and stole his only base on September 28, 1963.

3. Wills holds the NL record for being caught stealing seven seasons.

4. Lou Brock was caught 307 times.

5. Ty Cobb is the all-time AL leader with 46; Max Carey leads the NL with 33.

6. True. It is the AL record, set in 1969.

7. True. Vic Power of the Indians was the last to do it, in 1958.

8. Brock is the NL leader with 12 seasons of 50 or more steals.

9. Max Carey led the National League 10 times in stolen bases; Aparicio led the AL nine times.

10. False. Vince Coleman of the Cardinals stole 110 in his rookie season, 1985.

11. Davey Lopes is the NL leader with 38 steals without being caught; Willie Wilson and Julio Cruz share the AL record with 32.

12. d) Lou Brock

13. Lou Brock of the Cardinals stole 118 bases in 1974.

14. Rickey Henderson of the A's stole 130 in 1982, best season mark ever.

15. Rickey Henderson of the A's was caught stealing 42 times in 1982—the same year he set a record for most stolen bases.

16. Lou Brock, who stole 938 bases *en route* to the Hall of Fame

17. Rickey Henderson of the Oakland A's stole 100 bases in 1980.

18. Pepper—George Martin; Flying Dutchman—Honus Wagner; Minnie—Orestes Minoso; Ty—Tyrus Cobb; Fordham Flash—Frank Frisch; Snuffy—George Sternweiss; Pistol Pete—Peter Reiser

19. Tim Raines of Montreal and Vince Coleman of the

Cardinals

20. c) Harold Reynolds of Seattle, in 1987

Managers

1. Which major league managers have led the most different teams into the World Series:
   Dick Williams
   Joe McCarthy
   Bill McKechnie
   Casey Stengel
   Walter Alston
   Sparky Anderson

2. Who is the only manager ever to win a World Series in both leagues?

3. Which pitcher did the New York Mets trade to the Washington Senators to get manager Gil Hodges?

4. What San Diego broadcaster came out of the booth for the 1980 season and managed the Padres, then returned to broadcasting the following year?

5. Which of the managers listed below holds the record for most consecutive seasons with one team, and what is the record?
   - Casey Stengel
   - Connie Mack
   - Sparky Anderson
   - Walter Alston
   - John McGraw
   - Joe McCarthy

6. Who took over as manager of the Milwaukee Brewers in 1982, replacing Bob Rodgers, and then led the team to the AL pennant?

> KK. With first base unoccupied, an 0-and-2 pitch bounces in front of the plate. The batter swings and misses and the catcher catches the ball cleanly. Can the batter run to first base, or is he automatically out?

7. It should come as no surprise that Billy Martin, then managing the Texas Rangers, was the first AL manager ever booted out of both games of a doubleheader, but who was the first NL manager who got heaved by the umpires?

8. Match the real names with the nicknames of the major league managers listed below.

Jolly Cholly	Leo Durocher
Ol' Perfesser	Connie Mack
Little Napoleon	Whitey Herzog
El Senor	Ralph Houk
The Lip	Charley Grimm
White Rat	John McGraw
	Casey Stengel
	Miller Huggins
	Al Lopez

9. In 1961 and 1962 the Chicago Cubs went against the routine of having one man manage the team and hired a board of rotating coaches who consisted of which men?

10. Who is the only manager ever to win league/division titles with four different teams?
    Casey Stengel
    Bill McKechnie
    Billy Martin
    Walter Alston
    Earl Weaver
    Jimmie Dykes

11. What former major league manager was an All-American basketball player at Ohio State as well as one of the top sluggers during the sixties and seventies?

12. Who was the youngest person ever to begin the season as a major league manager, how old was he and what team did he manage?

13. Then there are the managers who have never won a pennant, such as two of the group listed below who have managed 15 or more seasons and hold the record for futility.
    Sparky Anderson
    Gene Mauch
    Jimmy Dykes
    Charley Grimm
    Connie Mack
    Bucky Harris

LL. The runner on first, with one out, attempts to steal second base and on a close play is ruled safe. But believing he is out, he gets up and starts for the dugout, and the second baseman runs over and tags him. How do you score the play?

14. Managers are hired to win, and two of the men listed below did it better in their respective leagues than anyone in history in leading their teams to pennants.
    Casey Stengel
    Joe McCarthy
    John McGraw
    Walter Alston
    Miller Huggins

15. Some major league teams seem to fall in love with their managers, such as the two listed below who hold the record for managing the same team the most times. Who are they, which teams and in what league?
    Jimmy Dykes
    Danny Murtaugh
    Bucky Harris
    Billy Martin
    Joe McCarthy
    Mel Ott

16. Which of the managers listed below has managed the most major league teams?
    Dick Williams
    Jimmy Dykes
    Billy Martin
    Bucky Harris
    Rogers Hornsby
    Charlie Dressen

17. Name the only National League manager ever to lead two teams in the same season, and how many times did he do it?

18. One of the most unusual deals in major league history involved a trade of which managers and what teams during the 1960 season?

19. Who was the famed Dodgers manager who graduated from the "Cradle of Football Coaches," Miami University in Oxford, Ohio?

20. Which of the managers listed below is the only one to have managed Hall-of-Famers Henry Aaron and Willie Mays?
    - Alvin Dark
    - Leo Durocher
    - Clyde King
    - Fred Haney

MM. A player is on the verge of breaking Lou Gehrig's all-time consecutive games played mark of 2,130 but twists his ankle in game 2,129 and is ruled out of any action the next day. Can he be announced as a pinch-hitter, which officially puts him in the game, and once announced, be replaced by another pinch-hitter and still get credit for a game played?

21. True or false: Manager Earl Weaver finished first or second in all but four of his seasons as Orioles manager?

Answers

1. Williams (Red Sox, A's, Padres) and McKechnie (Pirates, Cards and Reds)

2. Sparky Anderson, with the Reds (1975 and 1976) and Detroit (1984)

3. Bill Denehy was the pitcher-for-Hodges designee.

4. Jerry Coleman

5. Connie Mack managed the Philadelphia A's for 50 consecutive seasons, 1901–1950.

6. Harvey Kuenn

7. c) Mel Ott of the New York Giants on June 9, 1946

8. Jolly Cholly—Charley Grimm; Ol' Perfesser—Casey Stengel; Little Napoleon—John McGraw; El Senor—Al Lopez; The Lip—Leo Durocher; White Rat—Whitey Herzog

9. In 1961, the coaches were Vedie Himsl, Harry Craft, El Tappe and Lou Klein; in 1962, Tappe, Klein and Charlie Metro.

10. Martin won with the Twins (1969), Tigers (1972), Yankees (1976–77) and A's (1981).

11. b) Frank Howard, a two-time All-America cager for the Buckeyes in 1957 and 1958

12. Lou Boudreau was 24 years, four months and eight days old when he was appointed manager of the Cleveland Indians on November 25, 1941. He was also the team's starting shortstop.

13. Mauch, who starts his 27th season in 1988, and Dykes, who managed 21 years, never won a pennant.

14. Both McGraw and Stengel led the New York Giants and Yankees, respectively, to ten pennants. Ironically, Stengel played on one of McGraw's pennant-winners.

15. Billy Martin will begin his fifth stint as manager of the Yankees in 1988; and Danny Murtaugh managed the Pirates four times in 15 years.

16. Dick Williams and Jimmy Dykes managed six different major league teams.

17. Leo Durocher managed Brooklyn and the Giants in 1952; and the Cubs and Houston Astros in 1972.

18. Frank (Trader) Lane, GM of the Indians, traded manager Joe Gordon to the Tigers for manager Jimmy Dykes.

19. Walter Alston of the Dodgers graduated from Miami University.

20. c) Clyde King managed both Mays and Aaron.

21. True

Pennant Races

1. Relief pitcher Tug McGraw sounded what famous rallying cry for the NL champion Mets in 1973, and the world champion Phils in 1980?

2. What is the modern major league record—within five wins and losses—for the best season won-loss log for a second-place team?

3. Which major league team holds the season record for most wins, how many, and who were the four starting pitchers who accounted for 78 of the victories?

4. True or false: the New York Yankees were eliminated from the 1948 American League pennant race on the next-to-last day of the season by the Cleveland Indians.

5. True or false: The San Francisco Giants defeated the Los Angeles Dodgers on the final day of the 1982 season to allow the Atlanta Braves to win the NL-West title.

6. In 1982 the Milwaukee Brewers beat what team with whom they were tied on the final day of the season to win the AL-East title?

NN. Two strikes on the batter. On the next pitch, he takes a half-swing on a ball out of the strike zone. The ball eludes the catcher and the batter makes first base. But the plate umpire calls the pitch a ball and orders the batter to resume hitting. Can the batter appeal that pitch on the basis that he swung at the ball and ask for a third swinging strike?

7. What three National League teams were bunched within percentage points of each other on the final day of the 1956 season, and which team won the pennant?

8. How many games behind the Boston Red Sox were the New York Yankees when they began their surge to the AL pennant in 1978?

9. When the Detroit Tigers and Toronto Blue Jays met in the final weekend of the 1987 season, how many games in front were the Jays and what was the outcome of that three-game series?

10. In 1987 the Toronto Blue Jays led the eventual AL-East champions by how many games when the final week of the season began?

11. When the Phils defeated the Dodgers, 4-1, on the final day of the 1950 season to clinch the NL flag, which player drove in the winning runs in the 10th inning?

12. In 1985 the Kansas City Royals trailed by how many games in the AL playoffs before winning the pennant?

13. Who was the Yankee player whose home run won the 1978 playoff game against the Red Sox?

OO.	Runner on first, one out, and a hit-and-run situation, the batted ball hits the umpire, stationed at the front edge of the infield, on the fly, then carooms to the second baseman who catches it before it hits the ground. The fielder then throws to first to complete the double play. . .or is it?

14. In order to win the 1949 American League pennant the New York Yankees had to beat what team in the final two games of the season?

15. What National League team lost a 6½ game lead with 12 games to play in the 1964 pennant race?

16. What four American League teams were within percentage points of each other with two games to go on the final weekend of the 1967 season?

17. Whom did the Red Sox beat to cap their "Impossible Dream" American League pennant on the final day of the 1967 season, and who was their winning pitcher?

18. How many games out of first place were the New York Giants when they began their amazing run to tie the Dodgers for the 1951 National League pennant?

19. When the Red Sox and Indians staged their first American League playoff game in 1948, who was the starting and winning pitcher for Cleveland and whom did he beat?

PP.	A batted ball hits home plate and stays inside the foul lines. Fair or foul ball?

Answers

1. McGraw cried his famed, ''Ya' gotta have heart!'' as the relief ace for both teams.

2. The Chicago Cubs were 104-99 in 1909, 6½ games behind the Pittsburgh Pirates (110-42).

3. The 1954 Cleveland Indians won 111 games (in a 154-game season), and starters Bob Lemon, Early Wynn, Bob Feller and Mike Garcia had 78 of the wins.

4. False. The Red Sox eliminated the Yankees.

5. True

6. The Brewers defeated the Baltimore Orioles.

7. The Dodgers, Braves and Cincinnati Reds were all bunched together on the final day of the season, and the Dodgers won the pennant.

8. The Red Sox held a 14-game lead over the Yankees in August of 1978.

9. The Blue Jays had a one-game lead on Detroit, but the Tigers swept the three-game series to win the AL-East title.

10. Three and one-half games

11. Dick Sisler

12. The Toronto Blue Jays held a 3-1 lead over the Royals.

13. Bucky Dent

14. The Yankees had to beat the Red Sox, who held a one-game lead going into the final two games of the 1949 season.

15. The Philadelphia Phillies

16. The Red Sox, Twins, Tigers and White Sox—when there was no divisional play—were bunched to vie for the 1967 AL title.

17. The Red Sox defeated Dean Chance and the Minnesota Twins, and Jim Lonborg was the winning pitcher.

18. In mid-August, the Giants were 13½ games out of first.

19. Gene Bearden defeated the Red Sox and Denny Galehouse, 8-3.

Most of Hall-of-Famer Chuck Klein's 300 lifetime home runs were hit in this Philadelphia ballpark.

Oddities

1. What is the oddity in this inning of a 1959 game between Kansas City and the White Sox: Ray Boone reached first on an error; Al Smith reached first on an error; John Callison singled, scoring Boone; another error on that play scored Smith; Luis Aparicio walked and stole second; Bob Shaw walked to fill the bases; Earl Torgeson walked, forcing home Callison; Nelson Fox walked, scoring Aparicio; Jim Landis forced Shaw at home; Sherm Lollar walked, scoring Torgeson; Boone walked, scoring Fox; Smith walked, scoring Landis; Callison was hit, scoring Lollar; Aparicio walked, and Boone scored; Shaw struck out; Bubba Phillips walked, scoring Smith; Fox walked, scoring a pinch-runner; Landis made the final out.

2. On June 30, 1974, in the ninth inning of the second game of a doubleheader with the score 3-3 between the Mets and Cards in New York, Cleon Jones of the Mets hit a sinking liner to right field with runners on first and second and two

This park was named for one of baseball's all-time great managers.

out. Umpire Chris Pelekoudas ruled that the outfielder trapped the ball, and the runner on second scored the run. The Mets ran to their clubhouse, thinking the game was over. But the second-base ump, Peter Pryor, ruled the ball had been caught, ending the inning without a run. What happened?

3. True or false: The Chicago White Sox, during a game in 1962, were credited with three sacrifice flies in one inning.

4. Which team put together this record 10-run inning in the 1929 World Series, and who was the opponent:

   Al Simmons homered; Jimmie Foxx singled; Bing Miller singled; Jimmy Dykes singled, scoring Foxx; Joe Boley singled, scoring Miller; pinch-hitter George Burns popped out; Max Bishop singled, scoring Dykes; Mule Haas hit a three-run homer; Mickey Cochrane walked; Simmons singled; Foxx singled, scoring Cochrane; Miller was hit by a pitch; Dykes doubled, scoring Simmons and Foxx; Boley struck out; Burns struck out.

5. Who was the Japanese hitter credited with slamming more home runs than any pro player in the history of the game?
   a) Soo Zhu Ki
   b) Jim Shigeta
   c) Matsui Shigametsu
   d) Sadaharu Oh

6. Situation in two different games in the same decade: Runners on first and second base and the batter hits a screaming line drive. In those games, each first baseman makes the catch and turns in what identical play?

QQ. Runner on second and the batter breaks his bat as he hits a soft liner toward third. The ball, which surely would have short-hopped the third baseman, is struck by the flying end of the bat, and hits the runner before hitting the ground. Is the runner out? How about the batter?

7. What was unique about St. Louis Browns outfielder Pete Gray, who played just one season (1945) in the majors?

8. Name the two Heisman Trophy winners who also played major league baseball.

9. Mickey Mantle hit a home run in Washington that is unofficially listed as the longest in major league history and created the phrase "tape measure home run" because that is how it was measured. How far was it?
   a) 610 feet
   b) 595 feet
   c) 650 feet
   d) 565 feet

10. What former sportscaster from Des Moines went to California to cover the Chicago Cubs' spring training camp in 1937, and never left, except to take up residency in Washington in 1980?

11. Who was the centerfielder/third baseman for the Toronto Blue Jays who became a starting guard for the Boston Celtics?

12. Sandy Koufax pitched three no-hitters during his major league career, and one batter made the final out in two of them. Who was he?

13. Who was the Denver Broncos' all-pro quarterback who once signed a contract to play in the Yankees farm system, where he lasted just one summer?

RR. There is a runner at third, and the third base coach begins running around trying to distract the pitcher into commiting a balk or making a bad throw. What action can the umpire take?

14. What player appeared in two Cotton Bowl games with two different teams, and then hit more than 100 home runs in the major leagues?

15. This Cleveland player was the first Rookie of the Year ever to be sent to the minor leagues in each of the two succeeding years after receiving the award. Who is he?

16. Who was the All-American fullback from the University of California who was named the American League MVP in 1958?

17. The 1982 Milwaukee Brewers had a unique nickname modeled after their manager and their home run hitting prowess? What was it?

18. Who is the American League umpire who once wrestled professionally under the name, "The Hatchet Man," because he wore a black hood and carried an ax?

19. Wearing glasses is no big thing for a major league baseball player, but can you name the first catcher to do so, and the year he started?

20. A player named Larry Barton may hold the all-time record for frustration as a baseball player dreaming to get to the big leagues. What is it?

This National League park was famous for the upward slope of its outfield.

SS.	Bases loaded, two out. The hitter swings and trickles a ball down the third base line. The third baseman, running to field the ball, accidently kicks it into the catcher's glove in plenty of time for the force out at the plate. Is this a legal play?

21. Reggie Jackson had the nickname "Mr. October," because of his great clutch playing, yet he was really at his best, according to his lifetime statistics, before crowds in what range?
    a) 35–45,000
    b) 10–20,000
    c) 20–30,000
    d) 5–10,000

22. Can you name the only two managers after World War II who did not wear a team uniform in the dugout during a game?

23. How many American League players have hit four triples in a nine-inning game?

24. Listed below are players and their major league affiliations, but can you name the other professional sports teams on whom they played in the offseason?
    Chuck Connors—Chicago Cubs
    Dave DeBusschere—Detroit Tigers
    Ron Reed—Atlanta Braves
    Gene Conley—Boston Red Sox
    Bo Jackson—Kansas City Royals

25. Pete Alexander, George Case and Cal McLish are all former major league players, but can you name the Presidents of the U.S. after whom they were named?

26. What Kansas City A's shortstop played one inning at all nine

positions during a game in 1965?

27. Name this famous brother-sister tandem: He was a pitcher for the Giants in the late seventies and early eighties; she won more Wimbledon titles than any player in history.

TT.	In a National League game, the visitors have sent eight batters to the plate in the first inning, and it is the pitcher's turn to hit, with the bases loaded and two out. Can a pinch-hitter be used?

28. What Kansas City shortstop, first name U. L., gained some fame in the early eighties because he always chewed on a toothpick during the game, and what did his initials stand for?

29. Who is the popular sportscaster who once worked as a $200-a-month umpire, at age 21, in the Class A Midwest League?

30. Who is the New York Yankees outfielder who was also drafted by the ABA, NBA and NFL, though he did not play football at his alma mater, the University of Minnesota?

31. The great thing about the almost extinct doubleheader is being able to spend hour after hour watching major league baseball, except in St. Louis on September 26, 1926, and Brooklyn, on August 14, 1919, for what reason?

32. Speaking of time, how many minutes short of an hour, within five, are the records for both leagues for a nine-inning game?

33. Who is the only player to win Most Valuable Player awards in both leagues?

34. Baseball players and executives get some screwy nicknames. Match the player with the nickname:

Jim Dwyer	The Trader
Louis Novikoff	Sarge
Joe Medwick	Pigpen
Marv Throneberry	Toy Cannon
Frank Lane	Bruno
Tim Raines	Ducky
Tom Brunansky	Mad Russian
Jim Wynn	Marvelous Marv
Gary Matthews	The Rock

UU. The batter hits a home run to win the game, and touches every base until he gets to home plate where his delirious teammates mob him, and rush him to the dugout without him touching the plate. Under these circumstances is it still a homer if the missed tag is appealed by the defense?

35. Can you name the Hollywood actors who played the lead roles as baseball players in movies about the game:

Monte Stratton Story	Gary Cooper
It Happened One Spring	Robert Redford
Lou Gehrig Story	Paul Douglas
Babe Ruth Story	Jimmy Stewart
The Natural	William Bendix

36. Match these major league players with the colleges for whom they also were football stars:

Frank Frisch	Ohio State
Bo Jackson	Michigan
Sam Chapman	Fordham
Jackie Jensen	Stanford
Lance Parrish	Missouri
Phil Bradley	California
Vic Janowicz	Southern California
Chuck Essegian	Auburn

37. Who was the first batter in the first major league baseball night game?

38. Match the player and the foreign country in which he was born:

Grant Jackson	Dominican Republic
Elmer Valo	Holland
Bobby Avila	Venezuela
Bert Blyleven	Scotland
Bobby Thomson	Czechoslovakia
Luis Aparicio	Canada
Juan Marichal	Mexico

39. Can you match these mascots with their teams?

Phanatic	Atlanta
Chicken	Philadelphia
Chief Nokahoma	San Diego

40. Match these players with the colleges for whom they played baseball prior to a major league career:

Lou Gehrig	Columbia
Bo Jackson	Ohio University
Reggie Jackson	Texas
Roger Clemens	Arizona State
Frank Frisch	Auburn
Mike Schmidt	Fordham

41. Can you match the names of these famous shortstops with their retired uniform numbers?

Pee Wee Reese	33
Ernie Banks	11
Honus Wagner	14
Luke Appling	4
Luis Aparicio	1

VV.	A bit of chicanery. One out, a runner on second and the batter hits a long drive that the leftfielder snares while his glove is over the fence. Rather than showing the ball after the catch, he kicks the ground in disgust as if he should have caught it. The umpire, not seeing the ball, signals a home run, and as soon as the runner at second leaves his base, the fielder tosses the ball to the second baseman, who doubles up the runner. Does the double play stand?

42. Can you match the managers listed below with their uniform numbers, all of which have been retired?

Casey Stengel	1
Billy Meyer	14
Walter Alston	40
Lou Boudreau	37
Gil Hodges	24
Danny Murtaugh	4
Earl Weaver	5

43. Can you match these pitchers with their retired uniform numbers?

11	Sandy Koufax
16	Juan Marichal
17	Bob Gibson
19	Whitey Ford
27	Carl Hubbell
32	Bob Feller
45	Don Drysdale
53	Dizzy Dean

44. Match these famous first basemen with their retired jersey numbers:

Stan Musial	4
Lou Gehrig	3
Bill Terry	6
Hank Greenberg	5
Willie Stargell	8

45. Match these famous catchers with their jersey numbers:

Roy Campanella	32
Bill Dickey	5
Thurman Munson	8
Elston Howard	15
Johnny Bench	39

46. Match these famous third basemen with their retired uniform numbers:

Ken Boyer	19
Harmon Killebrew	3
Pie Traynor	20
Jim Gilliam	14
Brooks Robinson	(5)

47. Can you match the retired uniform numbers with these famous home run hitters?

3	Ted Williams
4	Mickey Mantle
5	Henry Aaron
7	Babe Ruth
9	Mel Ott
20	Joe DiMaggio
24	Willie Mays
44	Frank Robinson

48. The famed comedy team of Abbott and Costello had a great baseball comedy routine. Can you match the players and their positions which evoked so many laughs?

Oddities—Questions

Today	Pitcher
I Don't Know	Catcher
Who's	First Base
Tomorrow	Second Base
I Don't Give a Damn	Shortstop
What's	Third Base

Answers

1. Eleven runs were scored on just one hit.

2. The umpires ordered the Mets back onto the field to finish the game, though most of the fans had also left. The Cards won in the 10th inning.

3. True. Indians rightfielder Gene Green dropped two fly balls, which in the opinion of the official scorer should have been caught, that were ruled sacrifice flies. He also caught another fly for the first out in that unusual fifth inning, which was a "normal" sac fly.

4. The Philadelphia A's scored the record 10 runs against the Chicago Cubs and went on to win the Series.

5. d) Sadaharu Oh

6. George Burns of the Red Sox (1923) and Johnny Neun of

''Dem bums'' used to finish every season at this park with their patented promise, ''Wait till next year.''

the Tigers (1927) each caught the ball, tagged the runner at first before he could get back, ran to second and stepped on the bag before that runner could return, thus producing unassisted triple plays by a first baseman.

7. He was a one-armed outfielder, who played 61 games for the Browns and made only seven errors in the field.

8. Vic Janowicz of Ohio State (1950) and Bo Jackson of Auburn (1985)

9. d) 565 feet, at Washington's old Griffith Stadium on April 17, 1953, clearing the fence and finally rolling to a stop in the backyard of a house across from the ballpark.

10. Ronald Reagan, who was elected President of the United States in 1980 after a quarter century as an actor, and two terms as governor of California

11. Danny Ainge

12. Harvey Kuenn grounded out in Koufax's 8-0 no-hitter over the Giants in 1963; he also struck out for the final out in Koufax's perfect-game victory over the Cubs.

13. John Elway

14. Ransom Jackson played for TCU in the 1945 Cotton Bowl, and for Texas in the 1946 game. He hit 103 homers in ten seasons in the majors, playing for five teams.

15. Joe Charboneau, who won the award in 1980

16. Jackie Jensen of the Red Sox

17. The 1982 Brewers, managed by Harvey Kuenn, were known as "Harvey's Wallbangers."

18. Ken Kaiser

19. Clint Courtney of the Yankees in 1951

20. He played 25 years in the minor leagues (1932–56) and never played one game in the majors.

21. Mr. October did best in front of crowds of 10,000–20,000, hardly World Series attendance figures.

22. Connie Mack of the Philadelphia A's and Burt Shotten of the Brooklyn Dodgers

23. No one has ever done it.

24. Connors—Boston Celtics; DeBusschere—Detroit Pistons; Reed—Detroit Pistons; Conley—Boston Celtics; Jackson—Los Angeles Raiders

25. Pete Alexander was Grover Cleveland Alexander; George Case was George Washington Case; and Cal McLish was Calvin Coolidge Julius Caesar Tuskahoma McLish, a name that covered all historical bases.

26. Bert Campaneris played every position during a game against California on September 8, 1965.

27. Randy Moffitt pitched for the Giants and Billie Jean Moffitt King was America's greatest woman tennis player.

28. U. L. Washington was the Royals' toothpick-chewing shortstop, and those initials did not stand for anything—they were his given name.

The first night game played in this park resulted in a no-hitter pitched by the Reds' Johnny Vander Meer.

29. Brent Musberger of CBS

30. Dave Winfield was drafted by both the Utah Stars (ABA) and Atlanta Hawks (NBA), and by the NFL's Minnesota Vikings, all in 1973.

31. In St. Louis, the Yankees and Browns sped through a doubleheader in an AL record time of 2 hours, 7 minutes; and in Brooklyn, the Dodgers and Cubs got in two nine-inning games in 2 hours, 20 minutes. And no one asked for his money back!

32. The New York Giants beat the Phillies, 6-1, on September 28, 1919, in just 51 minutes; and the St. Louis Browns beat the Yankees, 6-2, on September 20, 1926, in only 55 minutes. Imagine, games under an hour in which 7 and 8 runs, respectively, were scored!

33. Frank Robinson won the MVP Award for Cincinnati (1961) and Baltimore (1966).

34. The Trader—Frank Lane; Sarge—Gary Matthews; Pigpen—Jim Dwyer; Toy Cannon—Jim Wynn; Bruno—Tom Brunansky; Ducky—Joe Medwick; Mad Russian—Lou Novikoff; Marvelous Marv—Marv Throneberry; The Rock—Tim Raines

35. Cooper—*Lou Gehrig Story*; Redford—*The Natural*; Douglas—*It Happened One Spring*; Stewart—*Monte Stratton Story*; Bendix—*Babe Ruth Story*

36. Frank Frisch—Fordham; Bo Jackson—Auburn; Sam Chapman—Southern California; Jackie Jensen—California; Lance Parrish—Michigan; Phil Bradley—Missouri; Vic Janowicz—Ohio State; Chuck Essegian—Stanford

37. Second baseman Lou Chiozza of the Phillies, who lost, 2-1, to the Reds in Cincinnati on May 24, 1935

38. Dominican Republic—Marichal; Holland—Bert Blyleven; Venezuela—Luis Aparicio; Scotland—Bobby Thomson; Czechoslovakia—Elmer Valo; Canada—Grant Jackson; Mexico—Bobby Avila

39. Phanatic—Philadelphia; Chicken—San Diego; Chief Nokahoma—Atlanta

40. Columbia—Gehrig; Ohio University—Schmidt; Texas—Clemens; Arizona State—Reggie Jackson; Auburn—Bo Jackson; Fordham—Frank Frisch

41. Reese—1; Banks—14; Wagner—33; Traynor—20; Appling—4; Aparicio—11

42. Stengel—37; Meyer—1; Alston—24; Boudreau—5; Hodges—14; Murtaugh—40; Weaver—4

43. 11—Hubbell; 16—Ford; 17—Dean; 19—Feller; 27—Marichal; 32—Koufax; 45—Gibson; 53—Drysdale

44. Musial—6; Gehrig—4; Terry—3; Greenberg—5; Stargell—8

45. Campanella—39; Dickey—8; Munson—15; Howard—2; Bench—5

46. Boyer—14; Killebrew—3; Traynor—20; Gilliam—9; Robinson—5

47. 3—Ruth; 4—Ott; 5—DiMaggio; 7—Mantle; 9—Williams; 20—Robinson; 24—Mays; 44—Aaron

When this stadium was built it was called the Big A; now it is home to which major league and NFL teams?

48. Who's on first; What's on second; I Don't Know's on third; Tomorrow is the pitcher; Today is the catcher; and I Don't Give a Damn is the shortstop.

Boxes Answers

A. The batter is out for interfering. The pitcher became an infielder when he stepped off the rubber, and the batter has no legal right to hit a ball thrown by an infielder.

B. No. No run can score on a a play in which the third out is a forceout.

C. The batter is given a single and only one RBI.

D. No. Though the batter is declared out, the play is a dead ball play, and the runner returns to first base.

E. No. He must stay in the game until the first batter is put out or reaches first base, or the side has been retired.

F. It is a foul ball. It is not legal to catch a ball in your hat.

This outfield wall was part of Boston's baseball scene for over fifty years. Its location now houses Boston University's athletic field.

G. Because the play was an appeal, the play was not a forceout situation. The runner did not have to leave to make way for the hitter, therefore the run counts because it was scored before the last out of the inning was recorded.

H. The run does not count. No run can score on a play in which the batter is out before he reaches first base, and the hitter never legally got there.

I. No. A player must be tagged with the ball, or with the glove when the ball is held securely inside it.

J. It is a fair ball.

K. No. No run can count when the third out is made by a batter before he reaches first base.

L. True

M. True. The rule finally was changed to its present version in 1926 after a pitcher, William Hubbell, was allowed by umpire Bill Klem to intentionally pass a hitter in this manner. The NL president, John Heydler, threatened to suspend the pitcher if he ever did it again, but Klem said the rules at the time were not specific. They were made so after that season.

N. The pinch runner gets credit for the run and the batter gets credit for the hit and RBI.

O. No. The ball is dead as soon as it strikes the batting helmet as it would be if it hit any foreign object in foul territory.

P. It's a double play.

Q. An earned run mark is figured by multiplying the number of earned runs by nine, divided by the number of innings pitched rounded off to the nearest whole number.

R. Yes. The umpire did not call time out. The batter is credited with a triple and scores on the throw to the plate.

S. None. The batter-runner was out the instant that he passed a preceding runner and became the third out before any of the other runners tagged home plate.

T. Yes. Normally no run can score after a third out, but this is an exception because: "The run would score on the theory that it was forced home by the walk and that all the runners needed to do was proceed and touch the next base." Since the runner from second did touch third before he was out, he complied with the rule, and all that happened thereafter was outside that play.

U. No. Because Adcock actually passed Aaron on the basepaths, he was out and had to settle for a double.

V. Out. While the ball is held securely, the base can be tagged with any part of the fielder's body, and the glove, on a fielder's hand, is considered part of the anatomy.

W. No. The second visit automatically means he's finished for the game, at any position.

X. No. The rules specifically forbid any headstarts of that type, and the runner is automatically out.

Y. No. The appeal must be made before the next play.

Z. No. When the pitcher became an offensive participant, the club lost use of the DH rule, and he and any subsequent pitchers must bat for themselves.

AA. Yes. The runner at second didn't have to go to third base, and his action cannot be held against the batter.

BB. It is a triple. An obstruction cannot prevent a batter from getting the full value from his hit.

CC. It is a foul ball. When an umpire calls "infield fly," he means "infield fly—if fair."

DD. The new baserunner is out because a hit batsman must touch first base, unless disabled, before being replaced by a pinch-runner.

EE. When the fielder dropped the ball, the runner was counted safe across the plate on his first trip.

FF. False. All defensive players except the catcher must be in fair territory at the time the ball is pitched.

GG. The runner is safe at first because once the batter is out, he no longer is forced to go to second base.

HH. The appeal came too late. It must come before the first pitch to the next batter in order for the first hitter to be declared out. However, the second hitter is replaced at the plate by the third hitter, who inherits his 1-0 count, and the leadoff hitter remains at first base.

II. Neither batter gets an official at-bat, and the pinch-hitter is credited with the walk and RBI.

JJ. That runner is out the instant he passed the base runner in front of him. The other runners can score legally.

KK. If the pitch hits the ground in this situation, the batter must be put out, so he should be on the move toward first.

LL. The runner gets credit for a steal, the out is ruled a pickoff, and the second baseman gets credit for the out.

MM. No. The announced batter must complete his time at bat—reach first safely or be put out— in order to prolong his playing streak.

NN. No. Only the defense can appeal a half-swing.

OO. No. If the umpire is in front of the fielders, the ball is dead, and the batter gets a base hit. Both runners are safe. If the ump is behind the infield the ball remains in play, but it is not a legally caught ball. The batter and runner must make their bases and they can be thrown out.

PP. Fair ball. Home plate is fair territory.

QQ. The runner is out, regardless of whether the ball hit the ground, because he was hit by a batted ball. The batter gets a single and first base.

RR. When a coach leaves his box and acts in any manner to draw a throw by a fielder, the runner must be called out. The coach is also thrown out of the game for such actions. . . both at the same time.

SS. Yes. The runner is out, and there is nothing illegal about kicking the ball.

TT. No. The pitcher must bat for himself in this instance. The pitcher listed in the batting order must pitch to one batter before he can be replaced.

UU. No. It's a triple. All the bases must be touched.

VV. Yes. If the ump reverses himself and rules a catch—and he must in this case—the runner must tag up before advancing. However, on this play, he can leave his base the moment the ball disappears from sight. If he did, it's *not* a double play. The burden is on the runner to play it safe.

Photos
Answers

Page 5: Yankee Stadium

Page 10: The Polo Grounds

Page 17: The Polo Grounds

Page 23: Seal Stadium in San Francisco

Page 28: Dodger Stadium

Page 35: The Coliseum in Los Angeles, which played host to 92,706 on October 6, 1959

Page 48: League Park

Page 55: Griffith Stadium in Washington, D.C.

Page 64: Sportsman's Park in St. Louis

Photos—Answers

Page 84: Forbes Field in Pittsburgh

Page 109: Baker Bowl

Page 112: Connie Mack Stadium in Philadelphia

Page 116: Crosley Field in Cincinnati

Page 126: Ebbets Field, home of the Brooklyn Dodgers

Page 129: Ebbets Field

Page 132: Anaheim Stadium is now home to the Angels and the Rams.

Page 136: Braves Field